Bouquets of Love

especially for

_____

_____

_____

_____

_____

_____

Bouquets of Love

Gifts from the heart

hm|books

hm|books

PRESIDENT Phyllis Hoffman DePiano
EXECUTIVE VICE PRESIDENT/CCO Brian Hart Hoffman
VICE PRESIDENT/EDITORIAL Cindy Smith Cooper
ART DIRECTOR Rachel Collins
COPY EDITORS Whitney Law, Maria Hopkins
ILLUSTRATOR Judy Jamieson

hoffmanmedia

PRESIDENT Phyllis Hoffman DePiano
EXECUTIVE VICE PRESIDENT/COO Eric W. Hoffman
EXECUTIVE VICE PRESIDENT/CCO Brian Hart Hoffman
EXECUTIVE VICE PRESIDENT/CFO G. Marc Neas
VICE PRESIDENT/FINANCE Michael Adams
VICE PRESIDENT/DIGITAL MEDIA Jon Adamson
VICE PRESIDENT/MANUFACTURING Greg Baugh
VICE PRESIDENT/EDITORIAL Cindy Smith Cooper
VICE PRESIDENT/CONSUMER MARKETING Silvia Rider

Hoffman Media
1900 International Park Drive, Suite 50
Birmingham, Alabama 35243
www.hoffmanmedia.com

ISBN # 978-1-940772-08-0

Printed in Mexico

Contents

Dedicated to my Mother, "Mimi,"
my daughter-in-law, Katie,
and my granddaughter, Amelia.

Introduction

Our bouquets of love come in many forms from the people in our lives. Whether it is a tiny bunch of flowers from the yard presented by a grandchild or a bouquet presented to a special mom by a bride on her wedding day, bouquets signify a special moment. Love bouquets come also in the form of a cup of tea or hot coffee when the moment calls for personal conversation. Each day is a gift, and we in turn give our time and attention to things that matter most in our lives.

I remember the first bouquet I received from my twin sons. It was the most beautiful gathering of dandelion blossoms from the yard. Their little weed-stained hands were chock-full of tender little stems holding their offering. Could there be anything more valuable to me? No, nothing. They thought of me and presented a love token to me.

Bouquets of Love celebrates the women in our lives and those who have made our lives richer. The floral bouquet is usually presented at a special time and signifies remembrance. We show our love bouquets by the deeds we do and the differences we make in the lives of those around us. Our mothers and grandmothers demonstrated their love with wonderful meals around the table, a special dessert, or time for listening and guiding.

This book presents thoughts and remembrances to celebrate our special women.

Phyllis Hoffman DePiano

A Mother's Heart

"*A mother is she who can take the place of all others but whose place no one else can take.*"

- Cardinal Mermillod

"If I had a flower for every
time I thought of
you...
I could walk through
my garden forever."

-Alfred Tennyson

"Children and mothers
never truly part —
bound in the beating of
each other's heart."

- Charlotte Gray

*A mother's hands are
welcoming, loving, and
comforting with just
the right touch.*

"When you are a mother, you are never really alone in your thoughts. A mother always has to think twice, once for herself and once for her child."

-Sophia Loren

"*A family can develop
only with a loving woman as its center.*"

-Karl Wilhelm Friedrich Schlegel

"But Mary kept all these things and
pondered them in her heart."
And such it is with mothers,
our wonderful memories can be tucked away
in our hearts to be relived over and over
again with the same joy.

-Luke 2:19 (NKJV)

"*Love as powerful as your mother's for you leaves its own mark. To have been loved so deeply, even though the person who loved us is gone, will give us some protection forever.*"

-J.K. Rowling, Harry Potter and the Sorcerer's Stone

"It is not until you
become a mother that
your judgement slowly
turns to compassion and
understanding."

-Erma Bombeck

Gifts from My Mother

Joys
of
Children

"*Little girls with dreams become women
with vision.*"

-author unknown

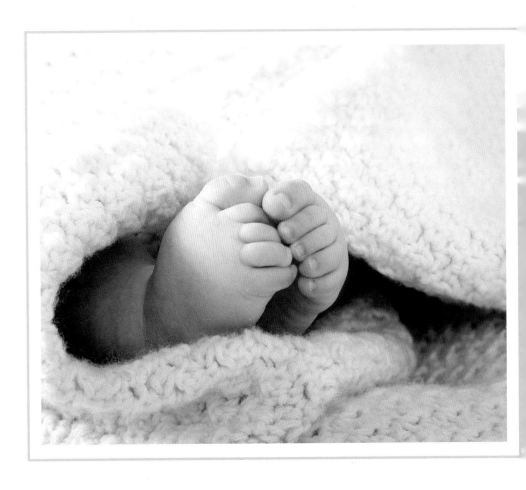

Children make our lives rich.
Their beautiful innocence
refreshes our souls.
Their smile melts our hearts.

Walk with me as I grow.
Watch me as I explore life.

Love me unconditionally.

When tiny hands deliver a
bouquet of freshly-picked flowers,
they deliver a bouquet of love.

"When I approach a child, he inspires in me two sentiments:

tenderness for what he is and respect for what he may become."

-Louis Pasteur

"We have to be patient with
ourselves and others.
Whether we're tending our roses
or raising a child, when we love life
and care deeply, we will be investing
our time wisely. In all important
matters, there are no shortcuts."

-Alexandra Stoddard in
her book *Time Alive*

"While we try to teach our children all about life,

our children teach us what life is all about."

-Angela Schwindt

"The children have been a
wonderful gift to me,
and I'm thankful to have
once again seen our world
through their eyes.
They restore my faith
in the family's future."

-Jacqueline Kennedy

*A child's eyes are the
windows to their souls.
Look into a child's eyes
to capture life from
their perspective.*

Jacqueline Kennedy once said,
*"If you bungle raising
your children, little else
that you do matters."*

"Childhood is a journey, not a race."

-author unknown

"Where you tend a rose, my lad, a thistle cannot grow," writes Frances Hodgson Burnett in *The Secret Garden*.

"*I want my daughters
to be beautiful,
accomplished and good;
to be admired,
loved, and respected;
to have a happy youth,
to be well and wisely married,
and to lead useful, pleasant
lives, with as little care and
sorrow to try them as God sees
fit to send.*"

-Louisa May Alcott
in *Little Women*

Fondest Childhood Memories

_____

_____

_____

_____

_____

_____

_____

_____

_____

_____

_____

_____

_____

_____

_____

_____

_____

_____

In Praise
of Home

"Whenever you are creating beauty around you, you are restoring your own soul."

-Alice Walker

"A house is made of walls and beams;

a home is built with love and dreams."

-William Arthur Ward

*A walk in the garden
with my mother
heightens my awareness
of colors, textures, and
the beauty of the world
through her eyes.*

*My mother's garden
beckons me.
The blossoms are
her children that she
nurtures and grows.*

One little flower can change an entire room.

I shall never forget the aromas
coming from my Mother's kitchen.
I can close my eyes and smell the
aroma of her scrumptious food.
I am home.

"Where we love is home —
home that feet may leave
but not our hearts."

- Oliver Wendell Holmes

*Home is your
sanctuary where you
can collect your
own thoughts
and enjoy solitude.*

*A charming quilt makes for a
perfect rainy day wrap.
A quilt reminds me of the
warmth of home.*

A trip to
Grandmother's
house is an
exciting time to
see her treasures.
For these treasures
tell the story
of her life.

"A house is much more than a mere shelter; it should lift us emotionally and spiritually."

-John Saladino

*A woman has the power
to turn ordinary into
extraordinary
in her home.
Celebrating life is
important every day.*

Coming home and
closing the doors
to the outside world
creates a haven
where family finds
restoration and renewal.

Favorite Family Heirlooms

_____

_____

_____

_____

_____

_____

_____

_____

_____

_____

_____

_____

_____

_____

_____

_____

_____

_____

_____

_____

_____

_____

Lessons
&
Prayers

There is a moment of transition so delicate that one hardly notices when a daughter becomes a best friend.

"But the fruit of the Spirit is love, joy, peace, patience, kindness, goodness, faithfulness, gentleness, self-control; against such things there is no law."

-Galatians 5:22-23

"There are two ways
of spreading light:
to be the candle or
the mirror that
reflects it."

-Edith Wharton

"Lord, make me an instrument
of Thy peace;
Where there is hatred, let me sow love;
Where there is injury, pardon;
Where there is error, truth;
Where there is doubt, faith;
Where there is despair, hope;
Where there is darkness, light;
And where there is sadness, joy.
O Divine Master, Grant that
I may not so much seek
To be consoled as to console;
To be understood as to understand;
To be loved as to love.
For it is in giving that we receive;
It is in pardoning that we are pardoned;
And it is in dying that we are born to
eternal life."

- St. Francis of Assisi

"Joy is prayer.
Joy is strength.
Joy is love.
Joy is a net of
love by which
you can catch
souls."
-Mother Teresa

"So now faith, hope, and love abide, these three; but the greatest of these is love."

1 Corinthians 13:13

"A thing of beauty is a joy forever."

-English Proverb

Prayer for My Mother

How thankful I am
for my mother.
May she know that
she is a gift to my life.
Her touch on my life
will transcend generations.
And her spirit will live
in all of us.

May my life be a
reflection of her love
that she has shared
with me all my life.
May she know that
my talents and creativity
are from her and that
she makes each day special.

At the end of my life
if I have been half the mother she is,
My children will have been lucky.
Her love knows no limit and
is unconditionally given.

Thank you God for this precious gift —
my Mother.

*Mothers and
Daughters
are closest when
Daughters become
Mothers.*

Prayer for My Child

*From the moment I knew
you were coming,
I knew life would be
richer every day.
Your eyes would reflect
a spirit of love.
Your heart tender with
compassion.*

*Thank you God for
this precious one
Who brightens the
hours of life.
May you bless this
soul with your love
and bring joy to
every day.*

"Trust in the LORD with all your heart, and do not lean on your own understanding. In all your ways acknowledge him, and he will make straight your paths."

-Proverbs 3:5-6

How powerful the phrase
"thank you"
when delivered with a
beautiful smile.

"*I remember my mother's prayers,
and they have always followed me.
They have clung to me all my life.*"

-Abraham Lincoln

Time
to
Share

When you have completed
a great book,
write a personal inscription,
and pass it on with
a note explaining
why you
loved reading it.
It will make for a
perfect conversation later.

Favorite Books

_____

Nothing replaces time invested
in the life of a person.

"*Happiness only real when shared.*"

-Christopher McCandless

The table is set with miniature cups anticipating the arrival of my granddaughter.
She brightens my day, helps me to see things very simply, and knows that she is the center of my attention for an afternoon.

"But I give best when I give from that deeper place; when I give simply, freely, and generously, and sometimes for no particular reason. I give best when I give from my heart."

-Steve Goodier

*Always make time
for a cup of coffee.
The details of your
missed schedule will
fade into beautiful
memories of time
well spent.*

When an occasion is
a lifetime event,
it is important that
we are there to
experience this milestone.
Being with a person
you love during a time of
extreme joy or
overwhelming sorrow
shows our
true devotion.

Children and Grandchildren

*Time spent
in meaningful
conversation will
become the memories
cherished forever.*

Most Cherished Conversations

Graceful Gratitude

"The love of family and the admiration of friends are much more important than wealth and privilege."

-Charles Kuralt

Nothing is more
appreciated than a
beautifully worded
handwritten
note of gratitude
or remembrance.

*A beautifully penned letter will change an
ordinary day into a glorious day.*

"Gratitude unlocks the fullness of life.
It turns what we have into enough, and more."

-Melody Beattie

Gentle words
carefully placed
convey gratitude for the
treasured gift of a friend.
Letters written
become revelations of
self-expression and
glimpses into the soul.

*"No matter how
busy you are,
you must take
time to make
the other person
feel important."*

-Mary Kay Ash

"As we express our
gratitude, we must never
forget that the highest
appreciation is not to
utter words but to
live by them."

-John F. Kennedy

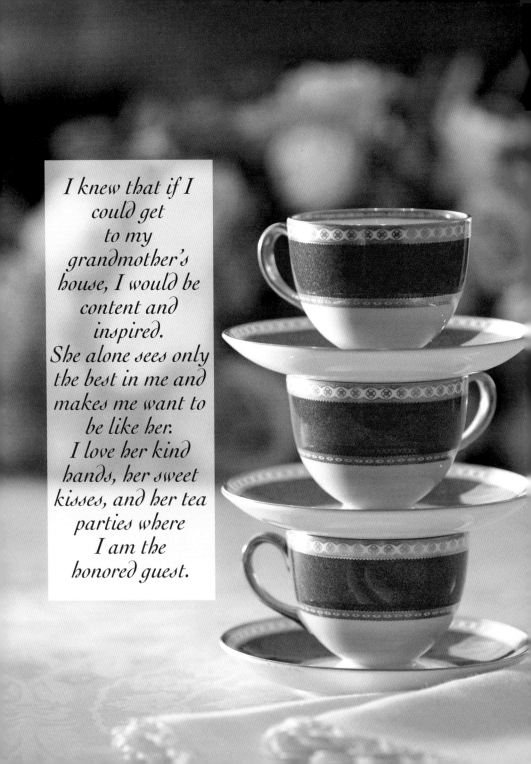

I knew that if I
could get
to my
grandmother's
house, I would be
content and
inspired.
She alone sees only
the best in me and
makes me want to
be like her.
I love her kind
hands, her sweet
kisses, and her tea
parties where
I am the
honored guest.

"Keep all special thoughts and
memories for lifetimes to come.
Share these keepsakes with
others to inspire hope
and build from the past,
which can bridge to the future."

-Mattie Stepanek

"If you are
really thankful,
what do you do?
You share."

-W. Clement Stone

Art of Gratitude

"I am only one,
but I am one.
I cannot do everything,
but I can do something.
And I will not let what
I cannot do interfere
with what I can do."

-Edward Everett Hale